MW01269124

TOM SELLECK:

Beyond the Stache - Exploring the Untold Journey

of Hollywood's Most Recognizable Icon

Joan A. Wilkerson

Tom Selleck

Tom Selleck

TABLE OF CONTENTS

Tom Selleck

INTRODUCTION

There are some names that stand out in the annals of Hollywood history and come to represent charisma, talent, and a lasting legacy. Among these greats is Tom Selleck, an actor whose image goes beyond performance to represent an icon, a gentleman, and a person whose very image has been ingrained in the minds of generations.

This book takes the reader on a deeper exploration of Tom Selleck's life, career, and mysterious persona. It is a voyage beyond the surface. Selleck has enthralled audiences for decades with his unquestionable charm, commanding presence, and, of course, his recognizable mustache, which evolved from just facial hair to a sign and emblem of his captivating attractiveness.

However, Tom Selleck is more than just the man with the fabled mustache. Beneath Hollywood's flash and glamor is a tale of tenacity, devotion, and an unflinching commitment to craft. Selleck's journey from modest origins to the pinnacles of celebrity is evidence of his drive, perseverance, and unwavering quest of perfection.

We go on a thorough examination of Tom Selleck's life through the pages of this book, covering everything from his early years to the height of his success and beyond. We explore the backstories of the parts, the incidents that molded his career, and the events that cemented his legacy. We discover the guy behind the famous mustache to find a complex person whose influence goes much beyond the big screen.

Tom Selleck

This goes beyond just narrating accomplishments or
providing a list of them in chronological order. It's a
personal portrayal, a patchwork of stories, observations,
and insights from people who have walked with him,
offering a peek at the person behind the mask.

We take a closer look at Tom Selleck's life in the
upcoming chapters, starting with his early years and the
people and things that influenced him. From the
impoverished areas of Detroit to the busy streets of
Hollywood, Selleck's story is one of tenacity, devotion,
and a steadfast love for his work.

We relive the iconic role of Magnum P.I., which thrust
him into the public eye and made the mustache an
integral part of the character. However, this book goes
beyond the obvious, examining the subtleties of Selleck's
career after Magnum and focusing on the parts that best
exhibited his range and sensitivity as an actor.

We discover the philanthropic and change-making side
of Tom Selleck, shining through the glitter of the

entertainment world. His extracurricular activities help to build a picture of a kind person whose influence goes well beyond the big screen.

Turning the pages will reveal candid observations and experiences from people who have worked with Selleck, providing insight into his principles, work ethic, and life lessons learned. These revelations provide a unique window into the true nature of the man behind the recognizable image, from triumphant moments to overcoming the obstacles that come with fame.

However, it's not only about the person; it's also about Tom Selleck's cultural influence on society. We go into the cultural significance of the mustache, its timeless appeal that never fails to enthrall viewers, and the ways in which Selleck's influence has made a lasting impression on popular culture.

More than just a biography, "Tom Selleck: Beyond the Stache" pays homage to an artist, celebrates a life devoted to storytelling, and delves into the life of a man whose presence has grown to be an essential part of our cultural fabric.

So allow this book to be your tour guide and traveling companion as you explore the lives and times of a real Hollywood great. Come along as we explore the stories, peel back the layers, and honor the man whose influence cuts across generations.

Welcome to the trip that explores Tom Selleck's heart and soul—beyond the stache.

CHAPTER 1: WHO IS TOM SELLECK

Celebrated American actor and producer Tom Selleck is known for his many performances in cinema and television as well as his unique charm and imposing presence. Thomas William Selleck was born in Detroit, Michigan, on January 29, 1945, and raised in Sherman Oaks, California. On a basketball scholarship, he studied at the University of Southern California, where he earned a business administration degree.

When Selleck first started his career in entertainment, he pursued tiny acting roles in TV series and commercials in addition to modeling. But what really shot him to fame was his breakthrough performance as Thomas Magnum in the popular television series "Magnum, P.I." (1980– 1988). Selleck's portrayal of the charming private detective in Hawaii, along with his trademark mustache, became synonymous with his persona and won him both critical and devoted admirers.

In addition to his Magnum achievements, Selleck demonstrated his flexibility in a number of TV and film roles. He starred in films like "Three Men and a Baby" (1987) and its follow-up, showcasing both his dramatic and humorous talents. His television performances include appearances in "Friends," "The Closer," and "Blue Bloods," where he has a recurring role as Frank Reagan, the father of a law enforcement family.

Over the course of several decades, Selleck has demonstrated both his dramatic talent and his lasting popularity as a leading man. His status as a Hollywood star has been cemented by his captivating charm, rich voice, and charisma on screen. In addition to his acting career, Selleck is well-known for his charitable work and dedication to a range of causes, which furthers his reputation as a kind person outside of the entertainment industry.

Tom Selleck is still regarded as a legendary figure in Hollywood, having made significant contributions to popular culture, television, and movies. His work as an actor, producer, and philanthropist has left a lasting impression on viewers all over the world, elevating him to a highly regarded and adored status in the entertainment business.

Tom Selleck's acting honors are not the only thing that characterize his lasting influence in the entertainment business. His innate charm and sincere demeanor have elevated him to a sought-after status and won him respect from both on and off screen. Over the course of his career, Selleck has successfully juggled high-profile parts with more introspective, character-driven ones, demonstrating his versatility as an actor.

Tom Selleck

Audiences with a wide range of preferences have come to love him because of his dedication to realism in his depictions, whether in thought-provoking parts, poignant comedies, or action-packed dramas. Selleck's reputation as a versatile and well-respected actor has been cemented by his ability to move between genres with ease and give powerful performances.

Outside of the theater, Selleck's charitable activities highlight his commitment to changing the world for the better. He has contributed to educational programs, supported veterans' organizations, and fought for environmental issues, among other charity causes. His dedication to giving back to society shows that he genuinely cares about issues that go beyond Hollywood's spotlight.

In private, Tom Selleck is renowned for leading a modest life, placing a strong emphasis on family values, and valuing his solitude. He is respected in the business and among his peers for his commitment to his work and his capacity to maintain perspective in the face of celebrity.

Tom Selleck is a timeless figure whose contributions to entertainment, charitable work, and ability to engage audiences through his performances have made a lasting impression on society. His legacy is still an inspiration to upcoming actors and a living example of the value of skill, commitment, and sincerity in the entertainment industry.

1.1 Early Life

Early childhood experiences laid the groundwork for the complex person who would go on to become a celebrity in the entertainment industry. Tom Selleck, soon after he was born, Robert and Martha Selleck moved to Sherman Oaks, California, where he spent his formative years.

Selleck attended Grant High School, where he excelled both academically and athletically, because of his childhood love of sports, particularly basketball. Because of his skill on the court, he was awarded a basketball scholarship at the University of Southern California (USC). While attending USC, he demonstrated his drive to succeed outside of sports by obtaining a degree in business administration.

Selleck spent his entire college career pursuing his love of acting. He joined the theatrical club and participated in several productions. However, he didn't seriously consider acting as a vocation until after working as a model and graduating from college. His formidable stature of 6 feet 4 inches (1.93 meters) and exquisite looks drew the attention of casting agencies, leading to his initial foray into small-scale television roles and advertisements.

Despite his early triumphs in the entertainment industry, Selleck found it difficult to establish himself as a well-known actor. He persisted in the face of numerous rejections and audition setbacks, steadily building his ability and portfolio. This period of perseverance and dedication would ultimately lead to his breakthrough role, propelling him to notoriety in a way that would define his career for years to come.

During Tom Selleck's childhood, a combination of physical endeavors, academic aspirations, and a developing interest in acting laid the groundwork for the diverse personality and skill set that would later define his career. His early life provided him with a solid foundation by instilling in him the values of tenacity, diligence, and a drive to be successful in his chosen career.

1.2 Influences

Numerous factors have influenced Tom Selleck's life and work, all of which have helped him develop as an actor, a public personality, and an honest person.

Grown in a loving and caring home, Selleck's childhood in Sherman Oaks, California, imbued him with a deep

sense of Midwestern family, community, and values. His
humility and sense of groundedness, which he carried
with him throughout his life and profession, were greatly
influenced by his family.

Selleck fell in love with acting while he was a basketball
scholarship student at the University of Southern
California. One of the biggest turning points in his life
was his choice to pursue drama instead of sports, which
led him to a vocation that would ultimately define him.

The direction he received at the Beverly Hills Playhouse
from renowned acting instructor Milton Katselas also
had an impact on Selleck's career. Selleck's attitude to
the art and the refinement of his acting abilities were
influenced by Katselas' guidance and instruction.

Selleck gained prominence after playing Thomas
Magnum in "Magnum, P.I.", which was his breakthrough
role. This well-known persona served as a
career-defining role for him in addition to showcasing
his acting prowess. Selleck's versatility as an actor is

Tom Selleck

demonstrated by his ability to play a variety of parts in both cinema and television, from serious dramas to lighthearted comedies.

Selleck's work ethic and personal principles served as strong foundations for his influences. Well-known for his diligence and dedication to excellence, he struck a balance between his personal and professional lives, winning the respect of his peers and the industry.

Even after becoming well-known, Selleck maintained her modesty and modesty. He placed more importance on keeping a low-key personal life and devoted himself to his work rather than the perks of celebrity. This strategy was intended to have an impact on how he handled the difficulties that came with becoming famous.

Selleck's impact goes beyond his own accomplishments. His mix of skill, commitment, and humility leaves an enduring legacy. He is an inspiration to people who want to succeed in life without compromising who they are, as well as to aspiring actors.

A variety of factors, including job decisions, mentorship, educational experiences, familial values, ethics, and a dedication to greatness, have influenced Tom Selleck. Together, these influences have molded him into the well-respected actor and person he is today, making a lasting impression on the entertainment business and encouraging others to follow their passions with sincerity and commitment.

1.3 Navigating the Path to Stardom

Tom Selleck's ascent to fame is evidence of his tenacity, fortitude, and unshakable dedication to his work. His early days in show business were characterized by the common challenges that actors in training experienced. Selleck was frequently turned down for roles during

Tom Selleck

auditions, but his perseverance and self-assurance kept
him focused on realizing his ambition of being an actor.

Selleck's breakthrough performance as Thomas Magnum
in the television series "Magnum, P.I." marked a turning
point in his career. This legendary role was both a
platform for his rise to prominence and a demonstration
of his acting abilities. Selleck became well-known
because of his portrayal of the endearing and tenacious
private detective against the alluring setting of Hawaii.

Alongside his magnetism on screen was the trademark
mustache that came to define Selleck's character. It
increased his allure and established him as a well-known
figure in Hollywood. A combination of good looks,
charisma, and the attraction of a mustache cemented his
status as a Hollywood star.

After "Magnum, P.I.," Selleck carefully considered his
employment options. Blockbuster movies and a variety
of television roles helped him to diversify his career. His
ability to play emotional roles as well as humorous

timing was seen in films such as "Three Men and a Baby," demonstrating his flexibility. This flexibility proved his versatility as an actor and made him more than simply the Magnum persona.

During his career, Selleck showed a thoughtful approach to choosing roles, striking a balance between roles that would help him achieve financial success and ones that would let him show off his range as an actor. He experimented with several genres, selecting jobs that pushed him and allowed him to show off different aspects of his skill.

Selleck's enduring significance extends beyond the pinnacles of his profession because he is still seen on television. Acting as Frank Reagan in "Blue Bloods" cemented his place in the industry's pantheon of legendary figures. His ability to adapt while remaining faithful to his roots and his everlasting charm are demonstrated by this attraction that spans generations.

Not only was Selleck able to take advantage of chances, but his ability to navigate the shifting tides of the entertainment industry was also a demonstration of his adaptability, perseverance, and unshakable commitment to his profession. His path to fame was marked by setbacks, victories, and a dedication to perfection that cemented his status as a dependable and well-liked character in Hollywood.

1.4 Early Years in Hollywood

Tom Selleck's early years in Hollywood were the result of his perseverance, life lessons, and the steady development of his entertainment business profession.

Selleck persevered despite initially having trouble with auditions and been turned down multiple times. He kept refining his skills, looking for new challenges and learning a great deal about how the business operated. In the beginning, he had modest parts in TV shows and advertisements, which gave him a platform to hone his talents and become more visible in the entertainment industry.

Selleck didn't really establish himself until he played Thomas Magnum in "Magnum, P.I.", which was his breakout role. Selleck's portrayal of the endearing private detective against the sun-drenched background of Hawaii made the series an instant hit and captured the attention of viewers all over the world. This crucial part not only catapulted him into celebrity but also marked a turning point in the development of his career.

With "Magnum, P.I."'s popularity, Selleck became a leading figure in Hollywood. His distinctive mustache and charismatic portrayal of the role made him a symbol that people adored and could not help but recognize.

After "Magnum, P.I.," Selleck deliberately tried to broaden his role repertoire as he navigated his career. He dabbled in television and movies, experimenting with different genres and demonstrating his range as an actor.

Tom Selleck

Films such as "Three Men and a Baby" demonstrated his comic flair, but other works emphasized his emotional versatility, solidifying his status as a versatile actor.

Selleck stayed committed to his work during his early Hollywood years, constantly improving his acting abilities and picking parts that allowed him to push his creative boundaries. His continued relevance in the industry was largely attributed to his dedication to authenticity and his readiness to accept a variety of characters.

Furthermore, Selleck's Hollywood career encompassed more than just acting. His creative reach in the entertainment industry was further extended when he delved into producing and directing.

His early years were marked by a combination of setbacks, successes, and an unwavering dedication to development. These encounters prepared the way for the long legacy of a multifaceted performer, a well-liked celebrity in Hollywood, and a memorable individual whose influence spans generations.

CHAPTER 2: MAGNUM P.I.: A BREAKTHROUGH ROLE

Tom Selleck's career was defined by "Magnum, P.I."; it was a turning point that propelled him to popularity and cemented his position as a major player in Hollywood. Selleck's reputation became inextricably linked to the renowned television series in which he played Thomas Magnum, leaving a lasting impression on the entertainment industry.

When "Magnum, P.I." debuted in 1980, it was set against the magnificent background of Hawaii and introduced viewers to Selleck's character, a charming and resourceful private investigator. The character captivated viewers' imaginations week after week with her easy charm, sharp wit, and tough yet refined personality.

Selleck embodied a combination of genuine fragility and sleek sophistication as Thomas Magnum, which made the character incredibly likable. Magnum's unique character and Selleck's magnetism on film combined to produce a compelling attraction that appealed to viewers all over the world.

The success of the program was largely due to Selleck's portrayal of the title character as well as its gripping mysteries and action-packed scenes. Magnum became more than simply a fictional investigator thanks to his unquestionable on-screen persona and easy mastery of the part. He even became a cultural icon.

Selleck's famous mustache, which became an essential component of Magnum's image, contributed to the character's unmistakable chemistry with Selleck. Selleck's inborn charm and the mustache enhanced the

Tom Selleck

character's allure, making him a legendary figure in the pantheon of television icons.

Selleck's career took off thanks to "Magnum, P.I."; it brought him critical praise, a passionate fan base, and a long-lasting legacy. The success of the show made Selleck a Hollywood starring man and catapulted him into the heartthrob category.

Beyond the honors and recognition, Selleck's career took a radical shift when he played Thomas Magnum. It confirmed his status as an actor who can command both small and large screens by showcasing his acting range, charisma, and natural talent.

In addition to solidifying Selleck's place in television history, "Magnum, P.I."'s lasting influence created the foundation for a career that would go beyond the confines of one iconic role, enabling him to take on a variety of characters and genres while always being connected to the fabled Thomas Magnum.

Tom Selleck

"Magnum, P.I." evolved into more than just a TV series, leaving a lasting impression on popular culture. Selleck's depiction of Thomas Magnum struck a chord with viewers, drawing in viewers of all stripes and cutting across demographic boundaries.

Selleck became a household name as the series' success catapulted him into the world of superstardom. In addition to receiving numerous nominations and awards, his depiction of Magnum won him a 1985 Golden Globe for Best Actor in a Television Series - Drama.

Beyond the screen, the show's popularity led to the creation of fan clubs, merchandising, and a dedicated fan base that embraced Magnum's persona as well as the actor playing it. Selleck's magnetic portrayal of Magnum elevated the character to a role of inspiration, perfectly capturing the essence of charm, wit, and intelligence.

Because it starred a Vietnam War veteran as the main character, "Magnum, P.I." was a historic turning point in television history. Acclaimed for its complex storytelling and social relevance, the show humanized the lives of soldiers while addressing timely topics of the day.

Even though "Magnum, P.I." was a huge hit, Selleck's professional path was not entirely determined by this legendary part. He made the most of the opportunity the show offered to experiment with other roles and endeavors, demonstrating his adaptability as a television and movie actor.

As evidence of Selleck's ability to create a character that lived beyond the television screen, "Magnum, P.I."'s legacy persists. Fans still find great pleasure in Tom Selleck's portrayal of Thomas Magnum, which not only epitomizes a period of television greatness but also marks a pivotal point in the actor's remarkable career. The part was a turning point in his career, bringing him into the public eye and creating the groundwork for a trajectory that still inspires and changes audiences today.

2.1 The Iconic Mustache

More than merely facial hair, Tom Selleck's trademark mustache is an iconic characteristic that has come to define his persona and greatly added to his appeal as a Hollywood star. With its unique look and appeal, the mustache was crucial in forming Selleck's character and had a long-lasting influence on popular culture.

The famous mustache's beginnings can be seen in Selleck's early acting career. Grown for a part at first, the mustache quickly became a distinguishing characteristic that helped him stand out in a field where top men frequently followed the convention of going unshaven. It was not planned; rather, it developed organically at the same time as Selleck's celebrity.

What started out as a decision to grow facial hair for a specific position in his profession eventually became an integral aspect of his persona. The mustache soon became well-known and a distinguishing feature of

Tom Selleck

Selleck's look, greatly adding to his rough allure and captivating charm.

The mustache had an impact that went beyond Selleck's personal appearance and turned into a well-known emblem on its own. It was welcomed by fans and admirers all over the world as a symbol of confidence, refinement, and masculinity. The appeal of the mustache crossed cultural barriers, connecting with viewers of all ages and lasting as a cultural touchstone.

Within the entertainment industry, the mustache developed to represent specific character traits such as the dapper leading man, the endearing investigator, and the pinnacle of masculine grace. It was clearly influential in creating Selleck's character as well as in determining what was considered to be a desirable and captivating male figure in popular culture.

The storyline surrounding Tom Selleck expanded to include the mustache, which gave his on-screen personas more mystery and appeal. It developed into an indispensable partner for the parts he played, giving each character's personality more nuance and individuality.

The mustache made a lasting impression on fashion, style, and society views of masculinity outside of the entertainment sector. Due to its ongoing popularity, fan tributes, imitations, and homages have become a cultural phenomenon.

The trademark mustache, which represents more than simply a physical characteristic but also a lifetime of charm, charisma, and self-assurance, continues to be an essential component of Tom Selleck's identity. Its enduring influence never goes away, cementing its status as a legendary cultural emblem connected to one of Hollywood's most renowned performers.

2.2 Behind the Scenes of Magnum's Success

Tom Selleck

"Magnum, P.I."'s popularity was a result of a number of behind-the-scenes factors coming together, rather than only being based on its captivating plot and endearing lead character. Its central theme was Tom Selleck's portrayal of Thomas Magnum, a figure who struck a profound chord with viewers all throughout the world.

The success of the show was greatly influenced by the casting process. Selleck was a wonderful fit for the role of Magnum, bringing the character's easygoing yet valiant manner together with his inherent charm, humor, and charisma. Magnum came to life in his presence, enthralling spectators and forging an instant bond.

Action, humor, and drama were all expertly woven together by a committed group of writers behind the camera. The show's writers' inventiveness and talent were evident in how well they were able to mix Magnum's daring adventures with poignant moments and complex puzzles.

Tom Selleck

Hawaii's stunning scenery functioned as more than just a backdrop; it was a key component of the show's attraction. The luxuriant scenery, stunning beaches, and lively culture gave the series a magical touch that improved its visual appeal and immersed viewers in Magnum's reality.

Another essential component to the success of the show was the chemistry between the cast members. The genuine chemistry and camaraderie that existed between Magnum, Higgins, TC, and Rick struck a chord with viewers and helped to sustain the show's long-term appeal.

Each episode was executed flawlessly because of the production crew's commitment and professionalism. The show's excellent production value can be attributed to the careful handling of every facet of production, including costumes, stunts, set design, and cinematography.

A perfect storm of components came together to make "Magnum, P.I." possible: an engrossing protagonist, gripping storyline, a stunning backdrop, harmonious ensemble cast chemistry, and a dedicated production staff. The popularity of the show was fueled by this synergy behind the scenes, which cemented its legacy in television history and left a lasting impression on viewers worldwide.

CHAPTER 3: POST-MAGNUM CAREER EVOLUTION

Subsequent to the success of "Magnum, P.I.," Tom Selleck made a conscious effort to broaden his roles and highlight his flexibility. After finding success on television, Selleck made the move to the big screen, showcasing his comedic abilities in hits like "Three Men and a Baby" and its follow-up. His ability to transition between media with ease while retaining his captivating charisma and on-screen presence was underlined in these films.

Tom Selleck

Selleck's post-Magnum career didn't end with movies; he kept fans enthralled with appearances on television as well. His portrayal of Dr. Richard Burke in the hit sitcom "Friends" demonstrated a distinct side of his acting abilities, endearing viewers as Monica Geller's more mature love interest.

A defining feature of Selleck's professional development was his exploration of a wide range of genres. With parts ranging from a police chief in the "Jesse Stone" TV movies to a Western hero in "Quigley Down Under," Selleck demonstrated an impressive range.

In addition to his playing career, Selleck also pursued directing and producing, broadening his artistic horizons in the entertainment sector. These behind-the-scenes positions further highlighted his diverse skill set and enabled him to contribute to the creation of interesting material.

Tom Selleck

Probably the most important turning point in his post-Magnum career was playing Frank Reagan on "Blue Bloods." Selleck returned to the small screen with this enduring program, playing a part that won him praise from critics. In addition to striking a chord with viewers, Selleck's portrayal of the father of a law enforcement family confirmed his continued significance in the television industry.

Selleck's exploration of a variety of roles, genres, and media throughout his career demonstrated his versatility and devotion to his profession. His reputation as a respected and adaptable personality in the entertainment world was cemented by his ability to move fluidly between comedy and drama, cinema and television, and always giving strong performances.

Following the enormous success of "Magnum, P.I.," Tom Selleck continued his career. His artistic journey was characterized by an unwavering search of diversity and a dedication to pushing himself creatively. He embraced a variety of characters and projects that demonstrated his range as an actor, stepping outside the parameters of his enduring TV role.

Selleck's move into filmmaking proved he could move between genres with ease. His roles reflected a range of moods and personas, from lighter comedies to severe dramas. His roles in films such as "Mr. Baseball," "In & Out," and "Runaway" demonstrated his talent for giving characters a genuine and nuanced sense of depth, enthralling viewers with each portrayal.

Selleck's artistic career continued to find substantial support on television. His roles in a number of TV shows and made-for-TV films gave him the chance to play complex characters that showcased a variety of his acting skills. His portrayal of the damaged police chief in the "Jesse Stone" series, in particular, became a hallmark part and demonstrated his ability to delve into deeply nuanced, introspective characters.

In addition to performing, Selleck's forays into producing and directing broadened his artistic interests.

Tom Selleck

His work behind the scenes on films such as "Reversible Errors" and "Monte Walsh" demonstrated his versatility and commitment to conveying stories from various angles.

His appearance on "Blue Bloods" signaled a big comeback to the forefront of television. Selleck's portrayal as Frank Reagan, the father of a law enforcement family, struck a chord with viewers and won accolades for its authenticity and complexity. His status as a television star was reinforced by the role, which also brought attention to his ongoing ability to engage audiences.

Tom Selleck's post-Magnum career demonstrated an artist committed to development and evolution by his willingness to explore a variety of roles, genres, and creative paths. His departure from the enduring Magnum role embodied a multifaceted performer fearless in self-improvement and in delivering shows that continuously moved audiences, cementing his reputation as a respected leader in the entertainment business.

Tom Selleck

3.1 Embracing Versatility

Tom Selleck's remarkable post-"Magnum, P.I." career
was characterized by a deliberate attempt to embrace
adaptability and investigate a broad range of parts in
various genres and media. After stepping away from the
beloved Magnum role, Selleck demonstrated his range
and depth as an actor by taking on a variety of roles in
movies and television shows.

When he entered the movie business, he played a variety
of parts, from dramatic to funny. Selleck's lighthearted
performances in films such as "Three Men and a Baby"
and its sequel captured audiences with his comedic
timing and charming demeanor. But his range went
beyond humor; in movies like "Quigley Down Under"
and "An Innocent Man," he showed off his dramatic
skills by playing characters with nuance and dignity.

Tom Selleck

Selleck's artistic style continued to find a substantial outlet in television. Especially noteworthy were his roles in a variety of TV shows and films, which demonstrated his ability to play nuanced, multifaceted characters. Selleck's ability to dive into complex, introspective parts is demonstrated in the "Jesse Stone" series, where he plays a tormented police chief battling personal demons.

In addition to his playing career, Selleck's production and directing credits reinforced his status as a versatile artist. His work behind the scenes demonstrated his dedication to narrative and his ambition to delve deeper into the realm of creativity outside of performing.

His appearance on "Blue Bloods" was the catalyst for a notable comeback on TV. Selleck demonstrated a distinct aspect of his acting talent as Frank Reagan, bringing nuance and realism to the role as the head of a law enforcement family. Viewers were moved by his performance, which demonstrated his ongoing capacity to establish a deep connection with audiences.

Tom Selleck

Tom Selleck's commitment to taking on a variety of roles and genres during his post-Magnum career demonstrated an artist not afraid to push himself. Beyond the boundaries of a single iconic role, his career revealed an actor dedicated to development, consistently making an enduring impression with his engaging performances.

3.2 Balancing Film, Television, and Personal Life

Tom Selleck's ability to preserve a feeling of harmony in the face of the demands of the entertainment industry is demonstrated by his ability to manage a successful career in cinema and television while also cultivating a meaningful personal life.

Selleck has demonstrated his versatility in both film and television throughout his career by flitting between the two mediums with ease. His methodical approach to roles allowed him to maintain a healthy balance between his personal and professional obligations while delving into a variety of personas, genres, and creative directions.

Despite the rigors of a demanding professional life, Selleck managed to find time for personal pursuits. He led a quiet life away from the public eye, placing a strong emphasis on family and moral principles. Well-known for his unwavering devotion to his wife Jillie Mack and their strong bond, Selleck balanced the demands of his professional life with his family.

He was devoted to his family even outside of his immediate vicinity. Selleck's philanthropic endeavors and participation in numerous charitable initiatives demonstrated his commitment to effecting positive change in the world outside of the glamour and flash of Hollywood. He demonstrated his dedication to giving back to society by actively supporting issues that were important to him, such environmental efforts and veterans' organizations.

Tom Selleck

Selleck was able to succeed in both his personal and professional lives by learning to compartmentalize and prioritize, even in the face of the difficulties associated with striking a work-life balance in the entertainment industry. In order to create a feeling of balance that allowed him to succeed in his job while nourishing his personal connections, he underlined the significance of upholding boundaries between work and personal life.

Selleck's ability to effectively manage his professional and personal lives is evidence of his fortitude, self-control, and appreciation for leading a balanced and satisfying life. His character, integrity, and commitment to what really counts in life are demonstrated by his ability to reconcile the demands of the entertainment industry with his personal obligations.

CHAPTER 4: UNVEILING SELLECK'S CHARITABLE CONTRIBUTIONS

Tom Selleck's charitable activities demonstrate his strong desire to have a good influence on a number of topics that are important to him. He has devoted time, money, and influence to a number of humanitarian causes during his career, exemplifying compassion and charity outside of the glamour of Hollywood.

Veterans' concerns is one of the causes Selleck is deeply committed to supporting. He has been a vocal supporter of veterans' organizations, valuing their service and fighting for their rights. Beyond only endorsing causes, Selleck's commitment to veterans' concerns goes beyond simple advocacy; he has taken part in activities,

generated awareness, and funded initiatives that help
veterans transition into life after the military.

Yet another area in which Selleck's altruism excels is
environmental conservation. His involvement in a
number of environmental activities is a result of his
dedication to protecting natural habitats and advancing
sustainability. He has used his platform to raise
awareness of the value of preserving the earth for
coming generations by supporting organizations that are
devoted to safeguarding wildlife, preserving natural
resources, and promoting environmental consciousness.

Selleck has shown his support for initiatives pertaining
to health and education. Having acknowledged the
transforming potential of these essential facets of human
growth, he has made contributions to initiatives that aim
to increase access to healthcare and education.

Beyond only providing financial support, Selleck's
charity donations extend beyond this; he actively
supports these causes by giving his time, voice, and

presence to occasions, campaigns, and projects that have the potential to make a positive difference. His public persona aside, his philanthropic endeavors are driven by a sincere desire to make a real difference in causes close to his heart.

Even though Selleck likes to keep his charitable activities low-key, his significant contributions have had a long-lasting effect on a number of organizations. His dedication to philanthropy is a reflection of his basic principles of compassion, empathy, and a desire to actually improve the lives of people. Selleck's charitable legacy is proof of the enormous influence that a single person can have on society via deeds of kindness and generosity, regardless of their position in society.

Beyond his public persona, Selleck's philanthropic involvement is a reflection of his own ethics and sincere desire to make a constructive impact on society. He frequently advocates for causes and participates in them firsthand, which increases the impact of his donations.

Tom Selleck

In addition to hosting events and giving speeches, Selleck has been actively involved in supporting causes related to veterans by collaborating with groups that provide assistance to veterans. His commitment to these causes is a result of his great admiration for veterans and his understanding of the difficulties they have after leaving the military.

Selleck is still greatly committed to the cause of environmental conservation. He regularly participates in conservation groups, working to protect natural areas and increase public understanding of environmental issues. His involvement includes campaigns that support environmentally conscious behavior and raise public awareness of sustainable methods.

Selleck also prioritizes healthcare and education in his charitable work. His contributions to healthcare, educational, and scholarship programs show a dedication to providing underprivileged people with opportunity for development, education, and access to essential resources.

Although Selleck keeps his charity low-key, his influence on the organizations and areas he supports is significant. His sincere desire to transform the world is demonstrated by his dedication to philanthropic initiatives that share his ideals and his commitment to bringing about positive change.

Selleck's altruistic deeds serve as a tribute to the enduring legacy that can be built via selfless acts of generosity and the transformational power of charity. His commitment to a number of causes shows how anyone, regardless of public standing, can have a significant and long-lasting influence on society by being kind, compassionate, and unwavering.

4.1 Insights into Tom Selleck, the Philanthropist

Tom Selleck

Tom Selleck has a strong sense of empathy and a sincere desire to make a positive difference in the world, which is evident in his charitable activities. Even though Selleck is well-known for his achievements in television and movies, he frequently makes silent charitable donations that are not seen by the general public.

His commitment to changing the world in areas that are very important to him is the foundation of his involvement in humanitarian endeavors. Selleck has a great deal of regard for individuals who have served their nation, which motivates him to support issues related to veterans. He directs his energy into programs that support, mentor, and provide resources to veterans in recognition of their sacrifices and as an advocate for their welfare.

Selleck places a high value on environmental conservation, as seen by his involvement in groups that work to protect natural areas and advance sustainable methods. Selleck's sincere passion for environmental concerns goes beyond simple lobbying; he actively

Tom Selleck

supports programs that strive to preserve ecosystems,
safeguard species, and increase public awareness of the
critical need of environmental preservation.

In addition, Selleck has a particular place in his
charitable activities for healthcare and education. His
backing of educational initiatives is to give people the
chance to grow and learn, enabling them to reach their
greatest potential. In a similar vein, his contributions to
healthcare projects demonstrate a dedication to
enhancing the accessibility of vital medical services and
resources for individuals who require them.

In addition to his monetary gifts, what distinguishes
Selleck as a philanthropist is his active participation and
sincere commitment to the causes he champions. He uses
his platform to raise awareness of important issues and
to magnify the voices of people calling for change, rather
than using it to gain personal recognition.

Even though Selleck would rather keep his philanthropic
activities private, his influence is widely felt in the fields

of education, healthcare, environmental protection, veterans' support, and more. His charitable legacy is a powerful illustration of the transformational potential of kindness, giving, and a steadfast dedication to changing the world for the better.

4.2 Public Persona vs. Private Life

Tom Selleck intentionally tries to preserve a sense of seclusion and normalcy away from the spotlight in his private life, which frequently contrasts sharply with his public persona as a renowned actor and cultural icon.

In the public eye, Selleck is renowned for his captivating on-screen persona, adaptable acting abilities, and memorable parts that have irrevocably changed the entertainment landscape. His role as Thomas Magnum in "Magnum, P.I." made him a television celebrity, and his box office triumphs in both movies and television confirmed his place in Hollywood history.

Tom Selleck

Under the spotlight of Hollywood, Selleck has an extraordinarily private life. He purposefully keeps his private life out of the public eye, stressing the value of privacy, family, and maintaining a feeling of normalcy away from the prying eyes of the media. Even with his notoriety, Selleck enjoys the peace and quiet of a low-key life. He frequently chooses to keep his personal life and charitable activities largely hidden from the public.

Selleck is devoted to maintaining his privacy even in his personal life. His commitment to preserving a solid and long-lasting relationship away from the paparazzi's gaze is demonstrated by his decades-long marriage to Jillie Mack. Together, they place a high priority on family values, highlighting the worth of their relationship and establishing a secure home for their loved ones.

Despite their significant influence, Selleck's charitable endeavors are frequently carried out in secret. He channels his donations and participation in philanthropic endeavors without pursuing public recognition, opting instead to concentrate on bringing about constructive transformations away from the harsh spotlight of the media.

The contrast between Selleck's public and private selves highlights his quest for balance in his life and his dedication to sincerity. Even though he enjoys the spotlight of the entertainment business, he appreciates his privacy, his personal space, and the ordinaryness of life away from the spotlight. The conscious division of the public and private domains is indicative of a profound comprehension of the significance of preserving one's identity and stability in the face of celebrity pressures. The fact that Selleck managed to maintain his composure in the face of fame is evidence of his honesty, modesty, and dedication to being loyal to who he is.

CHAPTER 5: SELLECK'S VENTURES OUTSIDE THE ENTERTAINMENT INDUSTRY

Outside of the entertainment industry, Tom Selleck has pursued a number of endeavors that are a reflection of his wide range of passions, interests, and spirit of entrepreneurship. His initiatives demonstrate his versatility and go beyond the glamour of Hollywood.

A noteworthy feature of Selleck's life apart from the entertainment industry is his enduring love of farming and ranching. He has invested a lot of time and energy into growing avocados on his avocado farm, which he owns and runs in California. His true interest in agriculture is demonstrated by his love of the land and dedication to sustainable farming methods, which he sees as a way of life rather than merely an economic endeavor.

Tom Selleck

Selleck has actively engaged in competitive activities and has a strong interest in sports. He is a skilled athlete who has a soft spot for volleyball. He was a founding member of the "Malibu Outdoor Volleyball Club," which dates back to the 1990s and reflects his passion for the game and desire to encourage sports outside of the entertainment industry.

Selleck has taken a chance on his entrepreneurial endeavors. He has invested in restaurants and undertaken other commercial endeavors. His entry into the culinary field is a reflection of his broad interests and his openness to investigating fields outside of entertainment.

Outside of his business endeavors, Selleck's dedication to philanthropy is a notable feature of his non-actor life. His commitment to having a significant impact on society is evident in his charity contributions, especially those that benefit veterans, the environment, education, and healthcare.

Tom Selleck

Selleck's forays into non-entertainment endeavors serve as a testament to his complex character, wide range of interests, and sincere dedication to goals that are consistent with his moral principles. His activities outside of acting, like as running his avocado farm, playing sports, learning about entrepreneurship, or supporting humanitarian organizations, perfectly capture the essence of a multifaceted person committed to improving many aspects of life.

Outside of the entertainment business, Tom Selleck pursues a variety of interests, including history and cultural heritage preservation. He has demonstrated a profound respect for historical relics and taken an active part in initiatives to advance historical consciousness and preservation.

Selleck's engagement with groups that protect historical sites and artifacts demonstrates his love of the past. He has backed programs designed to preserve historical sites and raise public awareness of their importance. His devotion to safeguarding cultural heritage is indicative of his desire to make sure that upcoming generations may access and value history's richness.

Because of his passion for writing, Selleck has investigated the literary world. In order to express his love of the Old West and to demonstrate his narrative skills outside of the movie theater, he wrote a number of Western books. His books offer readers captivating stories that blend history, adventure, and rich characterizations, all while showing his love for the American frontier.

Additionally, Selleck has provided the narration for documentaries, mostly historical in nature. His participation in historical films shows his dedication to teaching and enlightening viewers about important historical events, personalities, and cultural phenomena.

Tom Selleck is an actor, but his passion for history, literature, and preserving cultural heritage comes through in all of his endeavors. His varied pursuits outside of the entertainment sector demonstrate his curiosity for learning, his genuine dedication to making a positive impact in areas that are meaningful to him personally, and his passion for learning. Through these undertakings, a side of Selleck's personality that goes beyond his on-screen character is shown, presenting a complex person pursuing a wide range of interests and ambitions.

5.1 Influence and Impact Beyond the Silver Screen

Tom Selleck is a significant figure in many areas of society, and his influence goes well beyond the silver screen. His diverse achievements and long-lasting legacy include cultural influence, generosity, and serving as an example of timeless principles.

Selleck is a legendary personality in the entertainment business, and his impact goes beyond his level of fame. In addition to captivating audiences, his portrayals of

Tom Selleck

endearing characters—most notably, Thomas Magnum
in "Magnum, P.I."—served as role models, exemplifying
virtues like integrity, charisma, and bravery. Selleck
encouraged viewers to adopt the principles of respect,
loyalty, and tenacity in their own lives by
communicating these values through his performances.

Selleck's commitment to philanthropy is one of his
greatest legacies. His commitment to humanitarian
causes has positively impacted people's lives both
individually and collectively. These causes include those
that aid veterans, the environment, education, and
healthcare. His dedication to these issues demonstrates a
sincere desire to bring about improvement and act as a
spur for society advancement.

Selleck's legacy includes his classic mustache and
refined demeanor, which perfectly capture his essence of
masculinity and flair. He rose to prominence as a cultural
icon, personifying refinement, charm, and grace while
establishing ageless standards for fashion and
masculinity.

Beyond his public demeanor, Selleck exemplifies how to handle celebrity with humility and integrity by preserving a private life while juggling fame and normalcy. His conscious choices to put family, privacy, and a grounded life away from the spotlight first represent ideals that have a strong emotional connection with viewers all across the world.

Selleck is still influencing and inspiring people with his varied interests in history, literature, ranching, and entrepreneurship, among other things. His devotion to these projects shows a genuine desire to follow his passions outside of the worlds of celebrity and wealth, as well as a commitment to lifelong learning and discovery.

The effect and influence of Tom Selleck go beyond the entertainment sector. Beyond the silver screen, his legacy as an actor, philanthropist, cultural icon, and embodiment of timeless principles reverberates across society, creating a lasting impression and motivating future generations to uphold integrity, compassion, and a commitment to changing the world for the better.

5.2 Tom Selleck's Enduring Legacy

The long legacy of Tom Selleck is a tapestry woven with adaptability, morality, and a dedication to leaving a lasting impression both on and off screen. His impact endures beyond the glamour of Hollywood, making a lasting impression on generations and social classes alike.

Selleck's legendary depictions of people that epitomized charm, morality, and relatability are at the core of his reputation. From the daring nature of Thomas Magnum to other complex parts in movies and TV shows, Selleck created characters that connected with viewers and made an impact. Viewers were deeply impacted by his performances because of his ability to depict complex individuals and give them nuance and honesty.

Tom Selleck

Selleck's impact extends beyond the entertainment sector. His charitable endeavors, marked by a sincere dedication to causes near and dear to his heart, have made a noticeable and long-lasting difference. His commitment to helping veterans, fighting for environmental protection, advancing education, and funding healthcare programs demonstrates a history of empathy, compassion, and a desire to make a positive impact on the world.

Selleck had timeless principles, which is what made his legacy enduring. His devotion to privacy, modesty in the face of fame, and love for his family served as an example of how to handle celebrity with honor and dignity. His ability to strike a balance between his private and public personas demonstrates his strong sense of morality and groundedness.

In addition to his charitable and entertainment activities, Selleck has a wide range of interests in history, literature, entrepreneurship, and agriculture. His pursuit of passions away from the spotlight is a reflection of his curiosity, devotion to lifelong learning, and desire to experience different aspects of life outside of the movie industry. Tom Selleck is an example to others because of his lasting legacy. He embodies talent, morals, and a desire to have a positive effect. His impact is enduring, making a lasting impression on audiences all across the world.

CHAPTER 6: INTERVIEWS

Interviews with Tom Selleck provide a unique look into the man behind the famous personas he played on screen. In conversations, he exudes a mix of humility, wit, and sincere genuineness that gives listeners a glimpse into his complex character and moral principles.

Selleck is likable to interviewers and viewers alike because of his self-deprecating sense of humor and down-to-earth demeanor. His versatility in handling conversations is demonstrated by his ability to dive into more philosophical issues while yet engaging in lighter banter. His interviews are thought-provoking and enjoyable because he frequently blends comedy with intelligence.

The talks with Selleck emphasize his steadfast adherence to privacy and the purposeful division of his personal and professional lives. He is forthcoming and animated when talking about his work, but he keeps a respectful

Tom Selleck

distance when it comes to private affairs, stressing the value of shielding some facets of his life from the spotlight.

His interviews also provide him with an opportunity to talk about his charitable activities and raise awareness of subjects that are important to him. In addition to showcasing his art, Selleck takes advantage of these occasions to fight for causes close to his heart, including aiding veterans or protecting the environment.

Selleck's passion for a variety of topics outside performing is frequently evident in his interviews. He displays his passion and excitement for a wide range of topics, offering viewers an insight into his complex personality, whether he is talking about his literary ambitions, historical interests, or agricultural endeavors.

Interviews with Tom Selleck demonstrate his ability to handle the public eye with grace, humor, and sincerity. They offer insight into the thoughts of a gifted actor, a devoted philanthropist, and a complex person whose

Tom Selleck

depth and magnetism go far beyond the personas he
portrayed in films.

6.1 Personal Insights

Interviews and personal glances into Tom Selleck's life
have yielded a wealth of personal insights that provide a
deep grasp of life and the entertainment industry, along
with wisdom and morals.

Selleck's unwavering dedication to authenticity lies at
the heart of his personal observations. He frequently
stresses the value of remaining true to oneself in one's
personal and professional decisions. His counsel
frequently centers on the virtues of honesty, integrity,
and humility; he exhorts people to maintain their
integrity and sense of self in the face of celebrity
pressure.

Tom Selleck

Selleck frequently emphasizes the value of perspective and balance in his personal views. He advocates for the division of the public and private domains while managing the demands of celebrity. He talks on the value of family, privacy, and a balanced approach to life.

His insight encompasses the ideas of tenacity and welcoming difficulties. In his stories about his career in Hollywood, Selleck highlights the value of resiliency, diligence, and having an optimistic outlook in the face of adversity. His observations highlight the importance of viewing obstacles as chances for development and education.

Selleck frequently discusses the value of giving back to the community and having a significant impact on society in his personal musings. His dedication to charitable giving and support of different causes demonstrates a strong conviction that humanity has a duty to make a positive impact on the world.

Tom Selleck

Selleck's varied interests, which include a love of history, literature, entrepreneurship, and agriculture, are frequently reflected in his personal views. His reflections on these wide-ranging topics reveal his real enthusiasm for learning new things, his wonder about the world, and his genuine curiosity about studying all aspects of life.

A wealth of knowledge and moral principles can be found in Tom Selleck's own observations. His remarks reveal a depth of morality, honesty, and a genuine desire to uplift people by encouraging them to live real, fulfilling lives. Selleck shares timeless truths that ring true with audiences yearning for direction, motivation, and a greater comprehension of life's subtleties via his experiences and views.

6.2 Wisdom and Lessons from Tom Selleck

A multitude of life lessons gleaned from Tom Selleck's experiences, principles, and personal philosophy are encapsulated in his wisdom. His observations, which he frequently shares in interviews, public appearances, and windows into his personal life, strike a deep chord and provide timeless wisdom that transcends the entertainment industry.

The foundation of Selleck's teachings is authenticity. He promotes being real in both personal and professional interactions, stressing the value of remaining true to oneself. His guidance reflects his conviction that one should be authentic, rooted, and loyal to one's principles, encouraging others to celebrate their individuality rather than give in to peer pressure or expectations.

Another important lesson that Selleck conveys is the importance of striking a balance between celebrity and a private life. He emphasizes how important it is to preserve a sense of privacy, normalcy, and family in the middle of the glamour of celebrity. His focus on establishing a private life while juggling a public job highlights the significance of preserving equilibrium and perspective.

Resilience and persistence are important themes in Selleck's teachings. He discusses lessons learned from his time in Hollywood, emphasizing the need for perseverance in the face of difficulties and disappointments. The lessons imparted by Selleck emphasize maintaining a positive mindset, viewing setbacks as chances for personal development, and persevering in the face of hardship.

Additionally, Selleck's charitable nature teaches important lessons. His dedication to giving back and endorsing groups that share his ideals teaches us the value of empathy, compassion, and changing the world in a meaningful way. He emphasizes the value of giving back to society and exhorts people to use their riches and platform to bring about positive change.

Selleck's many interests in literature, history, and other subjects teach us the value of curiosity and lifelong learning. His support of life exploration emphasizes the importance of intellectual curiosity, lifelong learning, and a sincere love of a wide range of topics.

Tom Selleck's knowledge embodies priceless life lessons based on sincerity, fortitude, compassion, and a dedication to lifelong learning. His lessons are a lighthouse of wisdom, encouraging people to live authentically, face obstacles head-on, give back to the community, and have a well-rounded outlook on life.

6.3 Challenges

Even with his great success, Tom Selleck's journey has not been without difficulties. Despite receiving critical praise and playing famous roles, his Hollywood career wasn't without setbacks.

Striking a balance between his desire for a private life and his public character was one of the major hurdles Selleck had to overcome. As a well-known actor, it was difficult to preserve a sense of normalcy and privacy given the media's and the public's continual scrutiny. In order to maintain his status as a respected figure in the entertainment business, Selleck had to strike a careful balance between protecting his personal life and his career.

His renowned portrayal as Thomas Magnum put pressure on him to break out from typecasting, which made it difficult for him to pursue a more diverse career. Magnum, P.I. gave him enormous exposure and renown, but it also raised expectations that at first made it difficult to try out other kinds of jobs. Struggling to break through this barrier, Selleck progressively portrayed a variety of roles in television and movies to demonstrate his range as an actor that extended beyond the Magnum persona.

There were also difficulties due to the entertainment industry's dynamic environment. Resilience and flexibility are necessary to stay relevant over decades in a volatile sector by adjusting to shifting trends and

Tom Selleck

industry expectations. Selleck had to balance the
fast-paced nature of show business with his commitment
to creative principles.

Managing notoriety and privacy within the bounds of
public life posed constant difficulties. Selleck made an
effort to keep things regular, put his family first, and
respect privacy all the while meeting his obligations as a
professional and interacting with the public and media.

Selleck's path is a testament to his tenacity, fortitude, and
unshakable dedication to his trade. He overcame
obstacles in both his professional and personal life by
viewing them as chances for development and education.
This helped him forge a distinctive career for himself in
Hollywood while adhering to his morals and beliefs. His
ongoing success and stature as a recognized person in
the entertainment world are testaments to his ability to
overcome these obstacles with grace and resiliency.

Tom Selleck

6.4 Triumphs

Tom Selleck's long legacy as an entertainment industry
legend has been shaped by his numerous achievements
during his career in film, television, philanthropy, and
personal life.

Selleck's portrayal of Thomas Magnum in the television
series "Magnum, P.I." is among his greatest
achievements. In addition to launching him to global
acclaim, the role cemented his reputation as a TV idol.
His portrayal of the charming, Hawaiian-shirt-wearing
private detective won him praise from critics and a
passionate following from viewers all over the world.
His career took a significant turn when "Magnum, P.I."
became successful and brought him both an Emmy and a
Golden Globe.

In addition to his Magnum image, Selleck's
accomplishments include a smooth move into the film
industry, where he demonstrated his range as an actor.

Tom Selleck

His portrayals in films including "Three Men and a Baby," "Quigley Down Under," and "In & Out" demonstrated his ability to move between dramatic and humorous parts with ease, enhancing his reputation as a multifaceted actor.

One further achievement is Selleck's unwavering dedication to philanthropy. His support and activism for topics including healthcare, education, environmental conservation, veterans' affairs, and veterans' affairs have had a real impact on society. As a result of his engagement with nonprofits and commitment to bringing about constructive change, Selleck's humanitarian endeavors are a testament to his ability to make a significant impact outside of the entertainment industry.

One of Selleck's many achievements is his ability to maintain a strong dedication to family values and privacy while pursuing a prosperous career. He has managed to balance the demands of celebrity with a grounded personal life, putting his family and privacy first. This achievement is a shining example of honesty and resiliency.

Tom Selleck's successes span a wide range of endeavors in the entertainment sector, charitable giving, and moral rectitude. His continuing success and highly regarded legacy in the eyes of both fans and peers alike are a testament to his ability to captivate audiences, seamlessly transition between roles, make a meaningful contribution to society, and keep an authentic and balanced sense of self despite celebrity.

CHAPTER 7: THE MUSTACHE'S CULTURAL IMPACT

Beyond the realm of facial hair, Tom Selleck's famous mustache has gained cultural significance on its own. Selleck's identity was inextricably linked to his well-groomed mustache, which had a profound impact on fashion, trends, and ideas of masculinity in popular culture.

Since "Magnum, P.I." debuted in the 1980s, Selleck's mustache has been associated with tough charm and machismo. It was more than just facial hair; it was a distinguishing characteristic that enhanced his endearing personas. The mustache gained so much notoriety that it started to be seen as a representation of charisma and manhood, influencing fashion and grooming trends.

Selleck's moustache had a big influence on how society saw masculinity as well as style. It challenged social conventions and set a new bar for beauty, embodying the ideal of a tough yet polished masculinity. The mustache gained cultural significance and was frequently linked to charisma, confidence, and a carefree appeal.

Beyond just being visually pleasing, Selleck's mustache had a long-lasting impact on popular culture. It developed into an instantly identifiable brand that was frequently mentioned in parodies, mimicked by fans, and utilized as a characteristic in a variety of media. With its picture covering posters, memorabilia, and goods linked to Selleck's legendary roles, the mustache had a significant cultural impact.

Even after Selleck's on-screen persona ended, his moustache's lasting influence continued. It began to symbolize a bygone age of popular culture and television, giving rise to a sentimental icon. Even after "Magnum, P.I." came to an end, the mustache is still a recognizable and lasting part of Selleck's legacy, symbolizing a time in television history as well as a timeless combination of charm and manliness.

Tom Selleck

Tom Selleck's mustache evolved from facial hair to a cultural icon. Its influence on fashion, views of masculinity, and ongoing popularity in popular culture confirm that it is more than just a fashion statement; it is a timeless emblem of an era of captivating entertainment and a living embodiment of Selleck's legendary character.

7.1 Fan Tributes and Homages

Numerous fan tributes and homages have been inspired by Tom Selleck's ongoing popularity and famous roles, demonstrating the deep impact he has had on audiences of all generations.

Through a variety of channels, such as fan conventions, fan websites, social media posts, and fan art, fans honor Selleck. Fans paint elaborate portraits of Selleck's characters, especially Thomas Magnum from "Magnum,

P.I.," as a way to express their gratitude for the way he portrayed the role and the impact it had on them.

Fans can express their adoration for Selleck through social media. By exchanging cherished phrases, unforgettable moments, and anecdotes from his many roles, they help fans who like his work to feel more connected to one another. Regular trending hashtags honoring Selleck and his personas demonstrate the long-lasting influence he has had on mainstream culture.

Online forums and specialized websites are examples of fan-run projects that act as virtual meeting places for fans to talk about Selleck's career, trade trivia, and express opinions about his performances. Through these venues, fans may honor Selleck's accomplishments to the entertainment business and interact with like-minded others.

Fans can connect and celebrate their common enthusiasm for Selleck's work at fan conventions and get-togethers. These events provide fans a chance to

Tom Selleck

honor the career of their favorite actor and express their adoration directly through cosplay, panel discussions, and meet-and-greets.

In addition to these coordinated initiatives, people and organizations honor Selleck by copying his trademark mustache, dressing like his characters, or saying catchy quotes from his movies and TV series. These little actions demonstrate Selleck's everlasting influence on pop culture and his place in his fans' hearts.

Tom Selleck's admirers' homages and tributes to him bear witness to his enormous impact on audiences around the globe. They highlight his enduring impact in the entertainment industry and mirror the adoration, nostalgia, and gratitude fans have for his performances and the characters he brought to life.

7.2 Tom Selleck's Relationship with His Famous Facial Hair

One distinctive and distinguishing feature of Tom Selleck's character is his relationship with his well-known facial hair, especially his mustache. The well-groomed, thick mustache has come to represent Selleck's persona; it has transcended from a simple fashion statement to a deeply ingrained cultural icon.

Practical factors were the driving force behind the decision to sport the mustache at first. Selleck wore a thick mustache for the "Magnum, P.I." audition, which he kept for a theatrical part. In the end, this facial hair helped to define Thomas Magnum's character and became a crucial component of his audition appearance. Selleck's mustache was kept on for the program and quickly came to be synonymous with him.

With time, the mustache turned into a recognizable brand that influenced people's opinions of Selleck both on and off screen. It began to represent confidence, charisma, and masculinity in his roles. With the rise of Selleck's celebrity, his mustache gained notoriety as a distinctive representation of his character and attracted a devoted fan base.

There's more to Selleck's relationship with his well-known facial hair than meets the eye. Regarding the usefulness of the mustache, he has been open about how it became a part of his identity and how it frequently resulted in typecasting and fewer prospects for other jobs.

In spite of this, Selleck has continued to act modestly and with fun when discussing his mustache, frequently joking about how it has affected his reputation and career. He has periodically shaved it off for certain roles, showcasing his versatility as an actor and realizing the significance of his characteristic appearance at the same time.

The way Selleck feels about his well-known facial hair strikes a balance between its importance as a

Tom Selleck

distinguishing characteristic and his openness to change for the purpose of artistic expression. Even if his mustache is still a defining feature of his appearance, it doesn't fully capture the depth of his acting prowess or adaptability. Rather, it is a representation of a time period, a cultural icon, and a crucial component of Tom Selleck's ongoing entertainment legacy.

Tom Selleck

CHAPTER 8: SELLECK'S TIMELESS CHARM AND CHARISMA

The characteristics of Tom Selleck's persona that have enthralled audiences for decades are his ageless charm and charisma. His magnetic quality, which exudes from his demeanor, personality, and the characters he brings to life, is what makes him so alluring even beyond his basic screen presence.

His amiable demeanor and sincere warmth, both on and off screen, are essential components of Selleck's appeal. His ability to bring honesty and sincerity to his roles, whether he's playing a tough private investigator or a loving father figure, makes him likable to viewers. His easy ability to establish an emotional connection and evoke empathy in the audience is what gives him such a compelling charm.

Tom Selleck

Selleck's appeal is derived from his innate self-assurance and his easy fusion of tough masculinity and refined style. His distinctive mustache, which is a representation of his persona, heightens this allure and strikes a chord with viewers as a sign of tough yet sophisticated masculinity.

In addition to his physical qualities, Selleck's charm is emphasized by his wit, intelligence, and affable manner. His inherent appeal captivates audiences of all ages, regardless of their age or generation. His ageless charisma is on display as he delivers lines with a blend of charm, comedy, and depth.

Selleck's charm is also present in his off-screen presence, which combines grace, modesty, and a grounded demeanor. His interviews frequently display a humorous self-deprecation, showcasing a relatable and grounded attitude that connects with his audience.

Selleck's continued appeal and popularity are further testaments to his timeless charm. His fan following

Tom Selleck

continues to be loyal despite shifting entertainment trends and tastes, which is evidence of the lasting appeal of his charisma and the lasting effect he has made on audiences all over the world.

Tom Selleck exudes a timeless charm and charisma that come from a combination of relatability, confidence, genuineness, and a captivating presence that goes beyond the screen. It's a trait that endures, making a lasting impression on fans' hearts and solidifying his reputation as a charming and well-liked personality in the entertainment industry.

Tom Selleck's ability to project an air of relatability and authenticity is another source of his everlasting appeal and charisma. Selleck is sympathetic to audiences from a variety of backgrounds because, despite his fame, he keeps a friendly and humble manner.

His on-screen persona exudes a special fusion of assurance and vulnerability. Selleck gives his roles a real depth that connects with the audience, whether he's playing a resolute detective or a tender father figure. Because of his genuineness, the audience is able to relate to the roles he plays and become emotionally invested in the tales he narrates.

Selleck's charm goes beyond his skill as an actor. His public appearances, interviews, and off-screen encounters all exhibit a kindness and humility that adds to his attractiveness. His ability to participate in lighthearted banter and share personal tales, together with his sincere desire to connect with fans, further solidify the impression that he is a personable and relatable character.

The secret to Selleck's everlasting appeal is his capacity to change with the times without losing any of his timeless charm. Audiences of all ages are enthralled with his versatility as evidenced by his ability to adapt to a variety of roles and genres. Cast in serious parts, comedies, or action-packed adventures, he never fails to exude a magnetic charm that cuts across genre or time periods.

In addition to his genuineness and relatability, Selleck's ageless charm and charisma have cemented his status as a cherished personality in the entertainment business. His capacity to elicit strong reactions from viewers both on and off television is evidence of his enduring appeal and captivating charm, which has the power to enthrall viewers everywhere.

8.1 Fan Encounters and Stories

Fan interactions and tales about Tom Selleck attest to the continuing influence he has had on viewers; they frequently highlight the sincere bond fans have with him and the permanent impressions he left.

Many fans share accounts of their pleasant interactions with Selleck, praising his graciousness, compassion, and approachability. These stories frequently show how eager he is to interact with his followers, be it at fan events, autograph signings, or random meetings. Supporters often characterize Selleck as friendly, grounded, and truly grateful for their assistance.

Selleck's modesty and genuine personality are evident in several of the stories. Followers recall moments when he stopped to talk, smile for pictures, or share personal stories, leaving a lasting impression on those who were lucky enough to meet him. It is clear from his readiness to go above and beyond to establish a connection with his supporters that he genuinely values their support and affection.

Supporters frequently voice their appreciation for Selleck's kindness and commitment to philanthropy. Narratives abound on his philanthropic endeavors and his capacity to engage with admirers to lend support to projects that hold significance for them. This strengthens his reputation as a gifted actor who is also a kind person who is dedicated to changing the world.

These fan interactions and anecdotes frequently highlight the influence Selleck has had on people's lives outside of the screen. They demonstrate how his charm, generosity, and sincerity have made a lasting impression on everyone he has met, resulting in priceless experiences that go well beyond entertainment.

Interviews and anecdotes from fans with Tom Selleck reveal the enduring regard and admiration that they have for him. These stories emphasize Selleck's twin roles as a Hollywood celebrity and a personable, kind person, which strengthens the bond that has endured between Selleck and his dedicated following.

8.2 Tom Selleck's Impact on Pop Culture

Beyond his appearances in movies and television, Tom Selleck has had a profound influence on pop culture that permeates all aspects of society and permanently alters the cultural landscape.

Tom Selleck

Selleck's most notable contribution to popular culture is found in his iconic roles, especially in "Magnum, P.I." as Thomas Magnum. The role turned into a cultural phenomenon, catapulting Selleck to international renown and establishing a new benchmark for the sexy, charming detective genre. The recognizable red Ferrari, the Hawaiian shirts, and the mustache, of course, were icons not just of the show but of a time period as well, creating a lasting impression on viewers' collective memories.

Selleck is a symbol of a time in television history marked by legendary storytelling and larger-than-life characters, thus his influence goes beyond his individual roles. His appearance on film captured the essence of entertainment in the 1980s and 1990s, adding to the nostalgia for those years and evoking the spirit of the era.

He has become a cultural legend thanks to his persistent charm, charisma, and popularity. Beyond the screen, Selleck's effect can be seen in how people perceive masculinity, groom themselves, and adopt certain fashion trends. Symbolizing tough masculinity and refinement, the legendary mustache shaped grooming trends and became an integral part of Selleck's identity.

Selleck's lasting influence on popular culture is demonstrated by his significance in today's media and his long legacy. He continues to be praised, mocked, made reference to, and honored in a variety of entertainment mediums. His personas are regularly quoted or mimicked, and his trademark mustache frequently functions as a point of cultural reference in movies, TV series, and commercials.

Selleck's influence on popular culture is also a result of his charitable endeavors. His support of causes including healthcare reform, environmental preservation, and veterans' affairs has brought attention to these problems and motivated others to follow in his footsteps and effect constructive social change.

Tom Selleck's influence on popular culture goes beyond the entertainment industry. His legendary performances,

Tom Selleck

enduring charisma, classic style, and dedication to philanthropy have cemented his status as a cultural icon, setting precedents, swaying opinions, and leaving a lasting legacy that appeals to audiences of all ages.

CONCLUSION

"Tom Selleck: Beyond the Stache," it's evident that Selleck's impact transcends the confines of Hollywood, establishing a legacy that extends beyond his iconic facial hair. His enduring influence is rooted in a multifaceted career marked by versatility, integrity, and a genuine commitment to making a meaningful difference.

Looking ahead, Selleck's continuing legacy is poised to inspire future generations. His timeless charm, charismatic performances, and dedication to authenticity serve as guiding beacons for aspiring actors and individuals seeking to navigate the entertainment industry with grace and integrity. The lessons derived from his journey—be it his commitment to family, the balance he strikes between fame and privacy, or his unwavering dedication to philanthropy—remain invaluable guideposts for those aiming to carve their paths in an ever-evolving world.

Tom Selleck

Selleck's legacy extends beyond the realm of entertainment. His philanthropic endeavors and advocacy for causes close to his heart set a precedent for using fame as a platform for positive change. As he continues to champion charitable causes and inspire others to contribute to societal betterment, his impact will persist, leaving an enduring mark on the world beyond the silver screen.

The enduring allure of Tom Selleck lies not just in his on-screen persona but in the genuine qualities he embodies—a blend of authenticity, humility, resilience, and an unwavering commitment to values that resonate universally. His legacy will remain etched in the hearts of fans, serving as a reminder of the power of integrity, empathy, and authenticity in leaving a lasting impact on both the entertainment industry and society at large.

As the pages of this narrative close, Selleck's story continues—a legacy of timeless charm, enduring influence, and a commitment to making the world a better place. His impact will continue to shape

Tom Selleck

perceptions, inspire future generations, and stand as a
testament to the enduring power of an individual's
authenticity, both on and off the screen.

Made in United States
Troutdale, OR
11/28/2023

15056492R00056